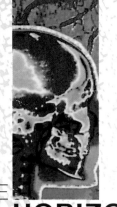

SCIENCE
HORIZONS

Life

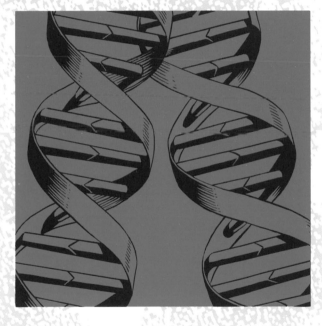

**ROBERT
SNEDDEN**

Chelsea House Publishers
New York • Philadelphia

First published in Great Britain in 1994 by
Belitha Press Limited, 31 Newington Green, London N16 9PU

This edition © 1996 Chelsea House Publishers
Copyright © 1994 Belitha Press Ltd
Text © 1994 Robert Sneddon

Library of Congress Cataloging-in-Publication Data
Snedden, Robert.
  Life / Robert Snedden.
    p.   cm. — (Science horizons)
  "First published in Great Britain in 1994 by Belitha Press
Limited"—T.p. verso.
  Includes index.
  ISBN 0-7910-3027-X. — ISBN 0-7910-3031-8 (pbk.)
  1. Life (Biology)—Juvenile literature.   [1. Life (Biology)]
I. Title. II. Series: Snedden, Robert. Science horizons.
QH501.S58   1995
                                        94-41163
                                        CIP
                                        AC

First printing
1 3 5 7 9 8 6 4 2

Manfactured in China

Editor: Neil Champion
Designer: Guy Callaby
Consultant: Christopher Cooper
Picture research: Dora Goldberg, Alex Goldberg
and James Clift of Image Select
Cover illustration: Neil Leslie
Other illustrations: David Pugh (pp 8-9, 32-33
and 40), Chris West (pp 10 and 16-17),
Kevin Lyles (pp 12-13 and 28-29) and
Guy Callaby/Dr. Barbara Mulloy (p42)

Picture acknowledgements:
Ann Ronan at Image Select: 14 right, 17, 18 top, 22
top, 23, 24 top, 25 left, 25 right, 26 top, 26 bottom,
27, 28, 30 top, 33 top, 35 right, 36.
Gamma: 32 (Dr. Per Sundstrom), 34 bottom (Jones
Spooner), 35 bottom (C. Voulgarapoulas), 35 top
(Jean-Luc Ducloux).
Images Colour Library: 7, 29.
Image Select: 20, 33 bottom.
Jacana: 4 left, 4-5, 14 left, 15 middle, 15 right, 21,
24 bottom, 32-33, 34.
Mary Evans: 19.
Microscopix: 30 bottom (Andrew Syred).
Planet Earth Pictures: 14 middle, 15 left.
Science Photo Library: 5, 6, 9 bottom, 9 top, 11, 16,
18 bottom, 22 bottom, 31, 39 bottom, 41 top, 42-43.
Special thanks to Francoise Mestre, Joel Pichon and
Julia Camlish for their assistance with illustrations.

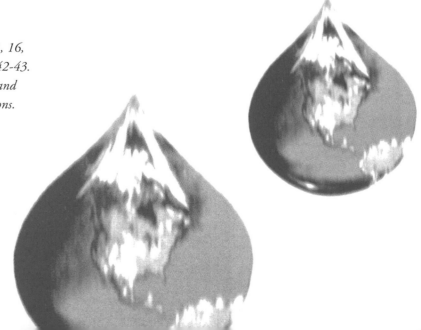

contents

4 **chapter one** Life forms

8 **chapter two** The beginning of life

16 **chapter three** Evolution

24 **chapter four** The structure of life

30 **chapter five** Into the nucleus

38 **chapter six** DNA

44 **glossary**

46 **index**

Life forms

The study of life is called biology. The word comes from the Greek *bios,* meaning life, and *logos,* meaning word or study.

Among the largest and longest-living of all forms of life are giant redwood trees. The ones shown here are in California.

Life is all around us. As living beings ourselves we are part of a complex web of life and we depend for our survival on a huge range of other living things that supply us with the food we eat and the oxygen we breathe. It sometimes seems that there is no end to the variety of forms life can take – from giant redwood trees 300 feet (100 meters) tall to microscopic bacteria; from whales swimming in the depths of the ocean to high-flying vultures.

These living things, or organisms, seem to be quite unrelated, yet at a deep level all life on Earth shares common characteristics. In this book we shall concentrate on finding out just what these characteristics are. The story that will unfold is of the way life changes and adapts. We shall look at some of the discoveries that have been made on the way to understanding how these changes work.

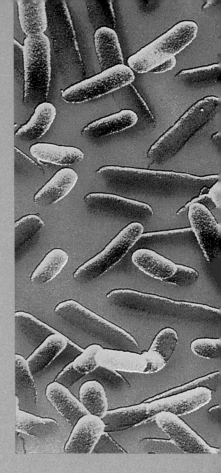

The smallest life forms are bacteria. There are many different kinds. The bacteria shown here are of a harmless type commonly found in human intestines.

Dividing up living things

We can divide up living things into different groups based on the features they have in common. For example, plants, animals and bacteria are particular groups. Large groups can be divided into smaller ones where more detailed similarities exist – plants can be divided into flowering and non-flowering varieties and animals into those with backbones and those without. The basic unit used in classifying is the species.

All living things are made up of cells. A cell is the simplest unit of life. Living things can be divided up according to the type of cells they have. The simplest cells are those of bacteria.

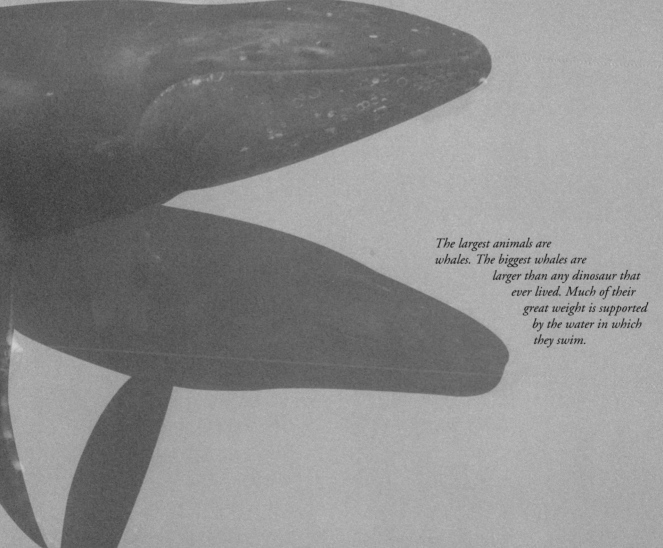

The largest animals are whales. The biggest whales are larger than any dinosaur that ever lived. Much of their great weight is supported by the water in which they swim.

The smallest bacteria can be one 10,000th of a millimeter across. There are many other one-celled, or unicellular, life forms. These are called protists and they have a more complex structure than bacteria. Then there are still more complex life forms, in which groups of cells act together as a team to their mutual advantage. Human beings are such a life form and are made up of billions of cells.

Identifying the simplest life form of all is difficult. Viruses exist on the borderland between the living and the nonliving worlds. A hundred times smaller than a bacterium, they cannot do anything except reproduce themselves. They cannot do this without first infecting a living cell and taking over its normal

Viruses exist in a shadowy borderland between the living and the nonliving worlds. They are simpler than bacteria and appear lifeless until they enter a living cell. Once inside they take over the normal processes of their host to make many copies of themselves.

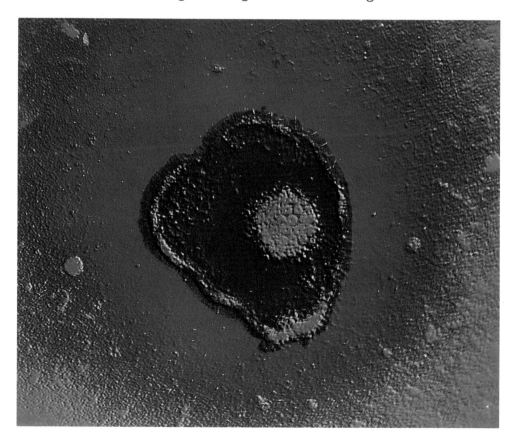

What is the difference between living and nonliving? This car production line is fully automatic and run by robots. It seems to do some of the things that living things do, such as taking simple materials and making them into something more complex. Yet we would not say that it is alive. It cannot reproduce itself or adapt readily to change, for example. Perhaps one day we may build machines that can do these things. Will they be alive?

processes. The combination of cell plus virus may be said to be alive, but outside a cell a virus is lifeless.

So if a virus isn't alive how do we define what is? There is no easy answer to this question. The answer, like life itself, is complex. Living things can take the nonliving materials around them and make them part of themselves. Living things can grow and reproduce and react to changes taking place around them. Living things have the capacity to change over long periods of time, adapting to changing conditions and giving rise to new forms of themselves.

DNA

The masterplan for all living things, which controls the way they will grow and develop, is held in a remarkable molecule – DNA. Using a simple code, DNA gives rise to all the complex forms of life we see around us. Every living thing has its own unique DNA and yet in every living thing DNA follows the same code and is fundamentally the same. This book is largely about DNA, the molecule at the heart of life.

The beginning of life

We may never really know how life began, but that hasn't stopped people from making all sorts of suggestions.

Many people believe that something as complex as life must have been created by an all-powerful supreme being. Such points of view cannot be discussed scientifically, however. Some people have suggested that life didn't begin on Earth at all but came here from outer space, perhaps in the form of bacteria or viruses carried on a meteorite. But if life didn't begin on Earth we still have to answer the question of how it began somewhere else. We wouldn't be any further forward.

Conditions for life

First let's try to imagine what conditions were like on Earth before there was any life. Four trillion years ago the Earth was a distinctly unpleasant place to be. It was a mere 600 million years old at this time and its surface was being constantly bombarded by the rocky debris left over when planets formed. Vast amounts of gas and steam poured out from hundreds of volcanoes, forming the Earth's first atmosphere. There was very little, or no, oxygen. As the Earth cooled, the steam condensed and fell in torrential rainstorms to form hot oceans. This must have been accompanied by spectacular lightning displays and continuous crashes of thunder.

Certain conditions had to exist before life, as we know it, could develop. The six chemical elements that are the basis of all living things – carbon, hydrogen, oxygen, nitrogen, phosphorus and calcium – had to be present. In the 1920s, the Russian scientist Aleksandr Oparin and the British scientist J.B.S. Haldane suggested that, under the right circumstances, such as those that existed on the early Earth, these elements would combine to form complex molecules called amino acids and nucleic acids. These molecules, as we shall see later, are vital ingredients for life.

In 1953, in a famous experiment, the American chemist Stanley Miller made a mixture of gases, thought to be similar to that of the early Earth's atmosphere, together with boiling water, in large glass flasks in a laboratory. By sending electric charges through the mixture to mimic lightning, he succeeded in making amino acids from the simple gases. This and later experiments showed that all the most important molecules that are part of living systems can be formed from simple starting materials.

Concentrations of amino acids and nucleic acids built up in the oceans in a sort of prelife "soup." In some way, no one is yet sure how, these giant molecules became organized into living organisms. The crucial development came when a

These are crystals of glycine, the simplest of the amino acids. The formation of amino acids in the early oceans was one of the first steps on the road to life.

The American chemist Dr. Stanley Miller with the equipment he used in a famous experiment to recreate conditions as they were in the early atmosphere and oceans of the Earth. He succeeded in making amino acids just as they may have been formed billions of years ago.

molecule appeared that could make copies of itself from the raw materials around it. A molecule capable of reproducing itself like this had a distinct advantage over those that appeared randomly. One of these self-copying molecules was DNA.

The odds of even the simplest form of life appearing in this way, purely by chance, are mind-numbingly huge, even larger than the chances of tossing a coin six million times and getting a head every time. But remember that it took many millions of years to happen and once the self-copying molecules had become established it wasn't just a question of chance. There was now a process of natural selection at work that pushed things along the right path and acted to preserve those changes that gave an advantage. Those molecules that could make many accurate copies of themselves would get the biggest share of the raw materials and would have the best chance of surviving.

One thing we can be certain about is that the very earliest forms of life got the energy they needed from the chemicals around them. As millions of years went by this source must have become increasingly scarce. A life form that could use another source of energy would have an advantage over the others. In the 1950s, geologists discovered microscopic structures in ancient rocks over three billion years old. These structures closely resembled life forms alive on Earth today. They were fossils of bacteria, including a type of bacteria called blue-green bacteria or cyanobacteria. What was important about them was that if they were like the present day cyanobacteria they would have been able to get the energy they needed by photosynthesis.

Photosynthesis

A step forward was taken by life when a means evolved of using the energy of the sun to power living processes. Photosynthesis involves the energy of sunlight being stored as chemical energy that can be used by the organism.

Carbon dioxide gas from the atmosphere is combined with water to form glucose, a simple sugar. As part of this process, oxygen is produced.

Oxygen was a deadly poison to the earliest organisms. It reacts very strongly with other substances and would have disrupted the formation of complex molecules that life depends on. Fortunately there was a solution to the problem. Three billion years ago the Earth's oceans contained a great deal of dissolved iron. The oxygen produced by photosynthesis was combined with this iron to form a now familiar substance – rust. Bound up with the iron, oxygen was now harmless. The nonsoluble iron oxide sank down and settled on the ocean floor. Over millions of years it formed rocks known as banded ironstone formations, or BIFs,

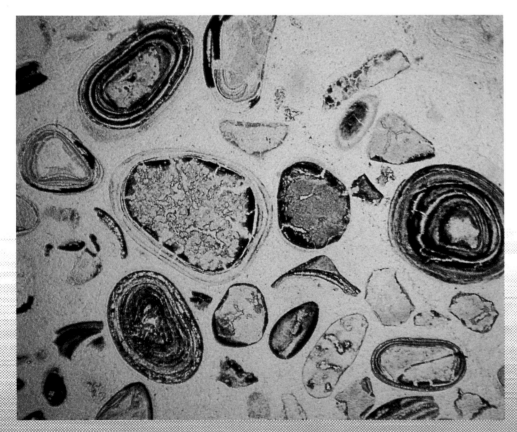

This thin slice of rock shows the fossil remains of tiny plants that lived around two trillion years ago. These plants got their energy from photosynthesis. In the process they released large amounts of oxygen into the Earth's atmosphere.

evidence today of the changes that occurred long ago. The oxygen-producing life forms were restricted to places where there was a supply of iron to combine with their oxygen. Some organisms retreated to places where there was no oxygen, such as the sediments on the seafloor. Bacteria that do not require oxygen to survive can still be found in such places today. As the levels of oxygen increased, organisms appeared that were able to tolerate it. Next, organisms began to put the oxygen to use in extracting energy more efficiently from their food.

The ozone layer

A great many people are concerned today about the ozone layer. This is like a shield in the upper atmosphere that protects us from the harmful ultraviolet (UV) radiation from the sun.

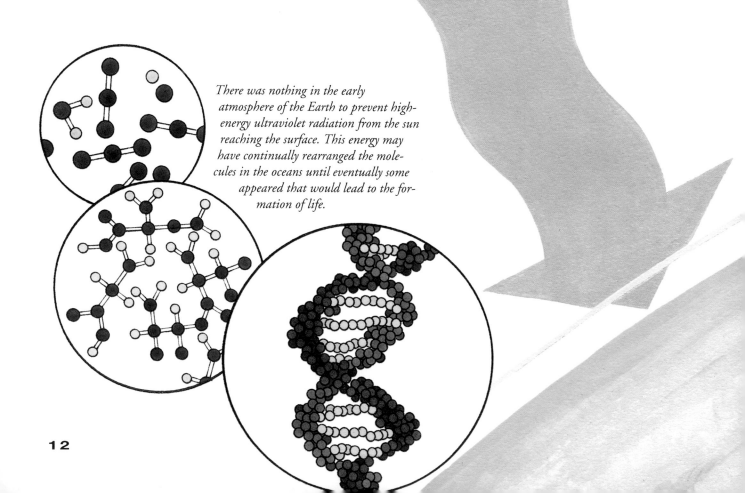

There was nothing in the early atmosphere of the Earth to prevent high-energy ultraviolet radiation from the sun reaching the surface. This energy may have continually rearranged the molecules in the oceans until eventually some appeared that would lead to the formation of life.

Over millions of years the amount
of oxygen in the atmosphere increased as
more was produced by photosynthesizing
organisms. In the upper atmosphere oxygen
was converted into ozone by the ultraviolet
radiation. This ozone shield absorbed
much of the UV radiation, preventing
it from reaching the surface where it
would have harmed the complex life
forms that were evolving.

Ozone molecule (O_3)

Ozone is a form of oxygen. When life was first becoming established on Earth there was no oxygen in the atmosphere and therefore there was no ozone layer. The surface of the planet was continually bathed in a level of UV radiation that would be deadly to almost all living things today. In a strange way this may have been a good thing. The energy from the UV radiation is thought to have been partly responsible for the continual rearranging of the molecules that eventually led to the appearance of life.

This is an artist's impression of how a forest may have looked around 300 million years ago. Coal was formed from the remains of trees such as this.

Below you can see two photographs of ferns. The one on the right shows a fossil over 200 million years old. The one on the left is of a living plant.

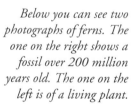

However, as life forms grew more complex, it became more and more likely that any random change would be harmful. Life developed in shallow waters, around 30 feet (ten meters) deep. Deep enough for the water to filter out the harmful UV rays, but not so deep that light couldn't get through for photosynthesis. As oxygen levels increased and the ozone layer began to form, life was gradually able to move into shallower and shallower waters. More and more new forms of life appeared, for example, corals, trilobites and early fish. It has been estimated that well over a thousand new animals, and probably many times more than that, evolved in the Earth's seas between 600 and 500 million years ago. There have been life forms that we shall never know about.

Life on land

It was then that the next great step was taken. By this time there was about a tenth of the present-day level of oxygen in the atmosphere. This was enough to provide a shield that would allow life to survive on the land. Evidence has been found that there were land plants by around 440 million years ago. Within a few million years the first land animals had appeared, looking something like present-day scorpions and millipedes.

One of the first land animals looked very similar to millipedes of today. The fossil remains on the left are around 500 million years old. On the right is a present-day living animal.

This fossilized trilobite lived 300 million years ago.

CHAPTER THREE

Evolution

The fact that we have found the remains of plants and animals that are no longer alive on the Earth shows that life has been changing since it first appeared.

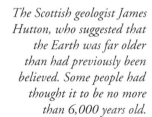

The Scottish geologist James Hutton, who suggested that the Earth was far older than had previously been believed. Some people had thought it to be no more than 6,000 years old.

The early life forms of almost four billion years ago have somehow given rise to the millions of different kinds of organisms that exist today, from simple bacteria to complex creatures such as ourselves. The process by which these changes have taken place is called evolution. What causes evolution to happen?

James Hutton

One of the first people to think seriously about evolution was the Scottish geologist James Hutton. He put forward an idea that was essential to its understanding. That idea was that the Earth had existed for far longer than had previously been believed. From his observations, it seemed to him that the Earth must be very old indeed. Just before he died in 1797, Hutton was working on a book about evolution by natural selection. No one examined Hutton's book until 1947, but this idea, later arrived at by others, was to become the cornerstone of evolutionary theory.

The French naturalist Georges Buffon thought that some creatures had changed from a perfect state to an imperfect one: for example, that donkeys were imperfect horses. The English doctor Erasmus Darwin carried on some of Buffon's ideas in a book called *Zoonomia*, written between 1794 and 1796.

Darwin suggested that changes could be brought about in a species by the influence of its environment.

The first big idea about the way evolution worked came from another French naturalist, Jean-Baptiste Lamarck. He suggested that the characteristics an animal or plant acquires during the course of its life could be passed on to its offspring. When Lamarck published his ideas in 1809, he gave the example of the giraffe. He suggested that if an antelope was fond of eating the leaves of a tree it would stretch its neck to get at as many leaves as possible. It would also stretch its legs to try and reach higher. As its life passed all this stretching would make its neck and legs a little longer. The antelope would then pass on its longer legs and neck to its offspring. The young antelopes would stretch even more and pass their still longer legs and neck on to their offspring. Eventually, through these gradual changes, a long-legged, long-necked antelope, that we call a giraffe, would appear.

The idea seemed plausible but it was wrong. There was no evidence at all that an organism could pass on an acquired characteristic to its offspring. There were also characteristics that Lamarck couldn't explain. For example, how could a stick insect try to make itself more like a twig and so improve its ability to hide from birds?

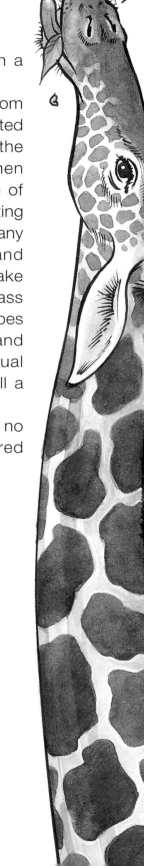

The French naturalist Jean-Baptiste Lamarck suggested that giraffes had evolved from antelopes that had stretched their necks during the course of their lives and passed on the longer necks to their offspring.

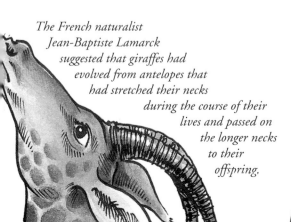

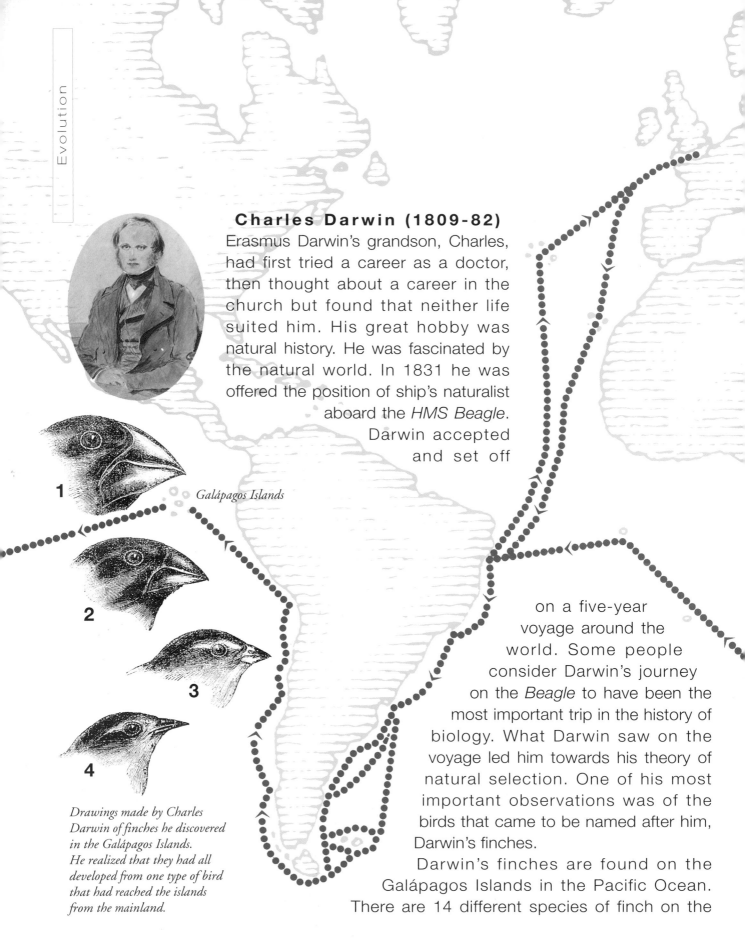

Charles Darwin (1809-82)

Erasmus Darwin's grandson, Charles, had first tried a career as a doctor, then thought about a career in the church but found that neither life suited him. His great hobby was natural history. He was fascinated by the natural world. In 1831 he was offered the position of ship's naturalist aboard the *HMS Beagle*. Darwin accepted and set off

Galápagos Islands

1

2

3

4

Drawings made by Charles Darwin of finches he discovered in the Galápagos Islands. He realized that they had all developed from one type of bird that had reached the islands from the mainland.

on a five-year voyage around the world. Some people consider Darwin's journey on the *Beagle* to have been the most important trip in the history of biology. What Darwin saw on the voyage led him towards his theory of natural selection. One of his most important observations was of the birds that came to be named after him, Darwin's finches.

Darwin's finches are found on the Galápagos Islands in the Pacific Ocean. There are 14 different species of finch on the

HMS Beagle, *the ship in which Charles Darwin voyaged for five years as ship's naturalist. The observations he made during that time were to lead him towards his theory of evolution by natural selection.*

island, all similar to each other in several ways. No other finch anywhere else in the world is like Darwin's finches. It seemed extraordinary to Darwin that 14 different birds that were found nowhere else could have arisen on this tiny group of islands. His explanation was that an older type of finch, the ancestor of the others, had somehow reached the islands from the mainland. Gradually the descendants of the original finches evolved to take advantage of the different conditions on the islands. For example, some developed powerful bills for crushing large seeds; others had narrow beaks for catching insects, and so on.

Darwin's books

What Darwin didn't know was what might have caused these changes. He returned to England in 1836 and prepared several books detailing what he had discovered on his journey. The first of these books, *A Naturalist's Voyage on the Beagle*, published in 1839, is a classic. It made him famous then and is still read today.

Shortly before his book was published, Darwin read a book that was to give him the inspiration he needed. This was Thomas Malthus' *An Essay on the Principle of Population*, first published in 1798. In simple terms, Malthus said that populations expanded until they outgrew their food supply. When this happened the

*Thomas Malthus
(1766-1834), whose book
An Essay on the Principle
of Population, published
in 1798, influenced
Darwin's ideas on
natural selection.*

weak died through starvation, disease or war, while the strong survived. Malthus was writing about human populations but Darwin saw how this principle could apply to all species. He thought that as species struggled to survive, "favorable conditions would tend to be preserved and unfavorable ones to be destroyed." The idea that things would get better belonged to Darwin, not Malthus.

Darwin knew that, for generations, farmers had selected the qualities they wanted in plants and animals. Sheep were bred to have thicker wool, cows to give more milk. Was there a force in nature that operated to select the species that were best suited to their environment? Darwin asked, "Can the principle of selection, which we have seen is so potent in the hands of man, apply to nature?"

Natural selection

Darwin decided that it could. He could see that individual characteristics of an organism – its height, strength, ability to react quickly, or to stay hidden – were vitally important in determining whether or not it would survive and have offspring. The better an organism was adapted to its environment, the better its chances would be of surviving to pass on its advantages. Every individual of each species had different characteristics of the species. Some might be tall, some short, some might be stronger than others, or able to jump higher. Because, as Malthus had pointed out, the Earth cannot support all the offspring produced by all living things on it, only those best fitted to their environment will survive. If the features that help them to survive are passed on to their offspring, then these features gradually become more common in the population as those members without them are weeded out. According to natural selection, the giraffe didn't get its long neck from stretching, as Lamarck suggested. Some antelopes were born with necks that were naturally longer than those of their fellows. The long-necked antelopes got more to eat, lived longer, and had more offspring. The offspring inherited the long necks from their parents. Over a long period of time the necks of successive generations would get longer and longer.

Natural selection could also explain how a stick insect might come to resemble a twig. An insect that looked only very slightly like a twig would have a small advantage over an insect that stood out against the bush they were sitting on. It would have a slightly better chance of escaping the notice of a bird. Therefore it would have a better chance of leaving descendants to inherit its sticklike appearance.

This stick insect may escape being eaten by a bird because its appearance makes it less noticeable. If it survives it can pass on its advantage to its offspring.

Alfred Russel Wallace, who developed a theory of natural selection at the same time as Darwin. The two men published their findings together.

In 1844 Darwin began to write a book on the subject. He took such care over it that he was still working on it in 1858. In that year the naturalist Alfred Russel Wallace sent a manuscript to Darwin for his opinion. To Darwin's great surprise he found that Wallace had come up with almost exactly the same theory of natural selection. Darwin made no attempt to publish his work first and claim the idea for himself. Instead, the two men agreed to work together on presenting a paper that summarized the conclusions they had both independently arrived at. Wallace never failed to give Darwin the credit for being the first to come up with the idea of natural selection and it is perhaps unfair that nowadays the theory is spoken of as "Darwin's theory of evolution" and Wallace is often forgotten.

Darwin gave up the immense book he was planning and wrote a shorter one instead. Published in 1859, it is one of the most famous books ever written and is called *On the Origin of Species by Means of Natural Selection, or the Preservation of Favoured Races in the Struggle for Life*, usually shortened to *The Origin of Species*. It is still in print today.

ON
THE ORIGIN OF SPECIES
BY MEANS OF NATURAL SELECTION,

OR THE
PRESERVATION OF FAVOURED RACES IN THE STRUGGLE FOR LIFE.

BY CHARLES DARWIN, M.A.,
FELLOW OF THE ROYAL, GEOLOGICAL, LINNÆAN, ETC., SOCIETIES;
AUTHOR OF 'JOURNAL OF RESEARCHES DURING H. M. S. BEAGLE'S VOYAGE ROUND THE WORLD.'

LONDON:
JOHN MURRAY, ALBEMARLE STREET.
1859.

The right of Translation is reserved.

A copy of the title page of the first edition of Darwin's most famous book.

Without doubt it was a book that changed the world. It started arguments that have lasted up until the present. For many it challenged the teachings of the Bible and threatened religious beliefs. In 1871, Darwin took the argument further when he published *The Descent of Man*, in which he showed that humans had evolved from other forms of life.

There were two things missing in the theory of natural selection. First, how did the variations between members of a species arise in the first place? Second, how were they passed on to the offspring? There was no reason why a long-necked antelope should not breed with a short-necked antelope. In which case, how long would the offspring's neck be? There had to be some mechanism that prevented the differences in neck length from being averaged out, otherwise there would never be any lasting changes and therefore no evolution. Unknown to Darwin, an Austrian monk called Gregor Mendel had come up with the answer to the second question shortly after the publication of *The Origin of Species* (see page 33). The answer to the first question would have to wait for almost another hundred years.

The origin of man?

Darwin's theories outraged many people when he published them. They saw them as a direct attack on their religious beliefs. Many believed that humans were special but Darwin's theory suggested that we were just another species of animal that had evolved from earlier animals. Darwin and his ideas were frequently ridiculed in cartoons such as the one shown below. Even today there are people who do not accept that Darwin was right.

CHAPTER FOUR

An illustration from an early study on the human body published in 1508.

The structure of life

Before we arrive at the answers to Darwin's problems, we will take a closer look at what makes up a living organism and at some of the steps that have been taken towards an understanding of how organisms function.

The study of the structure of living things is called anatomy. From the earliest times people have been aware that the bodies of larger animals are made up of a number of different organs. Inside a human body, for example, there are lungs, a heart, kidneys, a brain and several other organs. Each of the organs of the body has a job to do and they must all work together if the organism is to live successfully. Each of them is constructed in such a way as to be able to do that job and that job alone. The heart's job is to pump blood around your body. It couldn't take over the job of breathing for you if something happened to your lungs. Many animals have similar organs. Some animals have organs we don't have and some that we do have –

fish have gills for breathing underwater instead of lungs for breathing air, but they also have a heart and a brain, for example. Plants also have organs – their roots, leaves and flowers – which are completely different from an animal's organs.

In the photograph on the right, you can see the roots, leaves and flowers of a plant. These are its organs.

A late 15th century impression of how the Greek physician Galen (AD 129-199) may have looked.

The study of anatomy

One of the first people to make a serious study of anatomy was the Greek physician Galen, who died around 1800 years ago. He looked at various animals, including dogs, goats and monkeys, and (among other things) described the way that muscles work together in teams. Practically all European medicine for the next 1300 years was based on Galen's work. It was not until the sixteenth century that Andreas Vesalius, a Flemish anatomist, produced one of the greatest of all scientific books. It was called, in Latin, *De Corporis Humani Fabrica – On the Structure of the Human Body*. This beautiful book, published in 1543, showed the human body in natural positions and some of its illustrations are so exact that no other work has bettered it.

Investigations into the workings of life were transformed by the invention of the microscope at the beginning of the seventeenth century. One of the first people to put the microscope to this use was Marcello Malpighi, an Italian doctor. In 1660 he showed that blood flowed over the lungs through a complex network of tiny vessels. From this he guessed that air breathed into the lungs passed into these blood vessels and was then carried by the blood to the various parts of the body. Malpighi also discovered the smallest blood vessels of all, the capillaries. These were too small to be seen without a microscope and connected the smallest arteries to the smallest veins. This is how blood circulates around the body. We now know that after the body has taken the oxygen it needs from the blood in the arteries, the blood passes through the capillaries into the veins to travel back to the lungs to collect more oxygen.

Malpighi also made many important studies of other forms of life. He studied the way insects breathe, showing the tiny branching tubes inside their bodies that open out in tiny holes in the insect's abdomen. He was also the first to describe the tiny

Part of an illustration from the title page of Andreas Vesalius' great book On the Structure of the Human Body, *published in 1543.*

On the right are some drawings by Antonie van Leeuwenhoek, showing a few of the tiny living things he saw for the first time through his microscope.

openings in the under surface of plant leaves, called stomata. These are where a plant takes in the air it needs but Malpighi could not guess that.

Discovering the cell

The discovery that living things are made up of tiny individual units was made by Robert Hooke around 1665. He was examining a very thin slice of cork through a microscope and saw that the cork was made up of a pattern of tiny rectangular holes. He described them as "much like a honeycomb… these pores or cells, were not deep but consisted of a great many little boxes." Hooke's "little boxes" were actually the outermost boundaries of the once-living plant cells and were all that remained after the cell had died. The word, cell, was kept to describe the entire living cell, however, and is one of the most important terms in biology.

Another of the investigators using the microscope was Antonie van Leeuwenhoek, a Dutch amateur scientist. Van Leeuwenhoek kept a draper's shop, but his favorite hobby was exploring the world of the very small with microscopes he made himself. He looked at just about everything from tooth scrapings to pond water. He was the first to discover the tiny organisms called protozoa, in 1677. These were too small to be seen without the microscope. In 1683 van Leeuwenhoek made another great discovery. He described tiny structures that were at the absolute limit of the power of his microscope. From these descriptions we now know that what he saw were bacteria, the smallest of all living things. No one else would see bacteria for another hundred years.

A French doctor called Marie François Bichat first showed that each organ of the body was made up of different types of tissue in 1801. He called them tissues because they mostly appeared to be made up of flat, thin layers, like tissue paper. He identified 21 different sorts and showed that different organs were made up of

One of van Leeuwenhoek's microscopes. The single lens was held in a hole in the metal plate.

one or more kinds. Bichat lacked a microscope and could not investigate the detailed structure of the tissues. Each type carries out a particular function. For example, in your body nerve tissue carries messages and instructions from one part of the body to another, and muscle tissue makes your body move in response to these messages.

In 1838, the German botanist Matthias Schleiden made careful studies of different types of plant tissue under the microscope. He saw that all plants were composed of cells. The following year, 1839, Theodor Schwann, another German scientist, put forward the cell theory. In it he said that all living things are made up of cells or of material formed by cells and that each cell contains certain essential components. What these components are we will be looking at shortly. Because Schleiden had come up with more or less the same idea in connection with plants the previous year, both men are now given equal credit for the cell theory. Schwann showed that Bichat's tissue types depended on the kind of cells that made them up.

Single-celled organisms

The discovery of the cell was one of the most important in the entire history of biology. In 1845 Karl Siebold, a German zoologist, published a book that talked about the microscopically small protozoa that had been seen by van Leeuwenhoek almost 200 years earlier. Siebold showed that these were actually single-celled organisms. It seemed that an organism could be composed of just one cell. There are in fact many more single-celled life forms than there are any of the larger types.

In 1860 another advance was made when Rudolf Virchow, a German scientist who had been a fellow student of Schwann's, said that, "All cells arise from cells." For many centuries an argument had raged as to whether or not life could come from nonliving materials. This idea was called spontaneous generation. At one time people believed, for example, that maggots were generated by rotting meat, failing to connect the maggots with flies that landed on the meat. By the eighteenth century no one any longer thought that such things happened, but there was still disagreement as to how microorganisms appeared. It was thought there was some sort of "vital principle" in the air that bred microorganisms. Virchow's theory helped to put an end to such ideas.

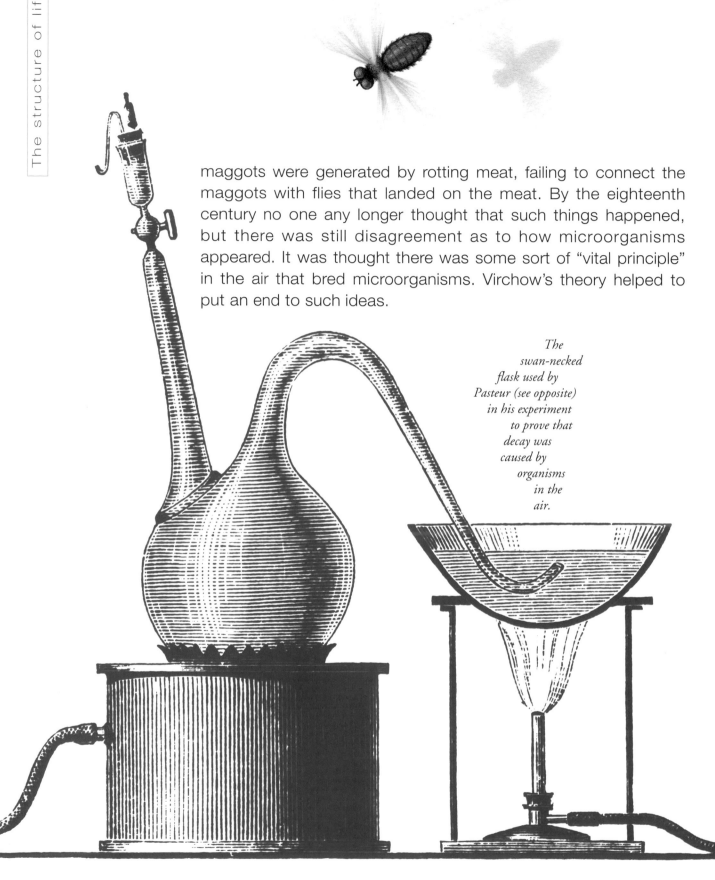

The swan-necked flask used by Pasteur (see opposite) in his experiment to prove that decay was caused by organisms in the air.

Bacteria in the air

At almost the same time, the French scientist Louis Pasteur carried out a series of beautifully simple experiments that proved that spontaneous generation was wrong. He showed that food went bad because it became contaminated by bacteria and other organisms that were carried on dust particles in the air. If you kept the organisms out you stopped the contamination. To prove this he first boiled some beef extract to kill off any organisms already present. He then left it in a flask at the end of a long, narrow, glass tube, shaped like the neck of a swan, that allowed air in but trapped any dust particles. The meat did not decay.

The germ theory

Pasteur also pointed the way towards a connection between the smallest and the largest living things. He believed that diseases could be passed from one individual to another by the tiny organisms, sometimes called germs, that caused the disease. This was his "germ theory of disease" and it is one of the most important ideas in the life sciences, particularly medicine. The germ theory encouraged other biologists to look more closely at bacteria, which were believed to be the carriers of disease.

One of these pioneers of bacteria studies was the German botanist Ferdinand Cohn, who published a three-volume book on bacteria. Cohn also made another very important discovery. He showed that the material inside a plant cell was virtually the same as that inside an animal cell. At a basic level it seemed that all the forms of life were linked. To see those links we will have to look into the cell itself.

People used to think that rotting meat made maggots. They didn't associate the maggots with the flies that landed on the meat and laid their eggs.

CHAPTER FIVE

Into the nucleus

One of the first people to recognize that cells had common features was the Scottish botanist Robert Brown.

Robert Brown (1773-1858), the Scottish botanist who was the first to see the nucleus of a cell.

He observed that all plant cells had a small body inside. In 1831, he named this feature the nucleus, from a Latin word meaning "little nut." The name has been used ever since. The nucleus is a vitally important part of the cell. We shall see why later. Finding out what is inside a cell is something of a problem. Although cells can vary greatly in size and shape, the biggest animal cells are usually no more than a tenth of a millimeter across. Anything small enough to fit into a cell is very small indeed. Another difficulty is that cells appear to be practically transparent when looked at under a microscope. Very little detail can be made out.

A way had to be found to make the inner parts of the cell show up. The answer came with the development of artificial dyes. In the 1870s, cytologists (people who study cells) began to experiment with these dyes. They found that different parts of the cell absorbed different dyes.

Using these staining techniques, the German scientist Walther Flemming made a study of animal cells. He discovered something inside the nucleus. Because this substance seemed to take up the dye he was using particularly well he called it chromatin, from a Greek word meaning color. When Flemming dyed a piece of growing tissue and looked at it under his microscope, he saw cells at various stages of division. He was able to sort out the order the stages came in. As the cell began to divide, the chromatin formed into long strands. In 1888, another German scientist, Heinrich Waldeyer, named these strands chromosomes, which means "colored bodies."

Chromosomes can only be seen when a cell is about to divide. These are from a fruit fly.

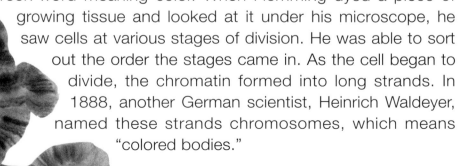

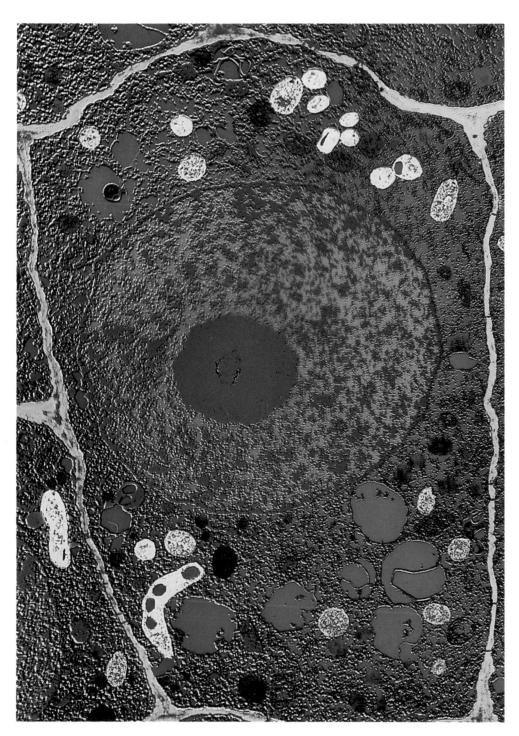

A single cell from the root tip of a maize plant. Plant cells differ from animal cells in having a thick cell wall round the outside. The large red and blue structure in the middle of the cell is its nucleus. This picture has been given false colors to make the different parts of the cell show up more clearly.

Just before a cell divides, the chromosomes appear from the nucleus and double in number (1). Each pair then lines up along the middle of the cell (2). Next the members of each pair are pulled towards opposite ends of the cell (3). Finally the cell divides and a new nucleus is formed in each of the new cells (4). Both the new cells have exactly the same number of chromosomes as there were in the original cell.

1

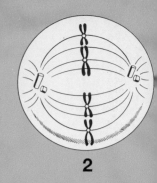

2

These chromosome strands always seemed to be present when cells divided and Flemming called the process of division mitosis, from the Greek word for thread. As the cell division progressed, Flemming saw that the chromosomes doubled in number. They were then pulled apart – half went to one end of the cell and half to the other. Next the cell divided, leaving each of the two new daughter cells with an equal amount of chromatin as the chromosome strands disappeared back into the two new nuclei that formed. Flemming published his findings in 1882 but he was not aware of how significant they were.

A few years later Edouard van Beneden, a Belgian cytologist, followed up Flemming's work. In 1887 he showed two important facts about chromosomes. First, every cell in an organism had the same number of chromosomes, and second, that number was the same for every member of a particular species. For example, every healthy human cell has 46 chromosomes. Van Beneden then observed that when sex cells were formed, the chromosomes did not double in one division of the cells. Sperm and egg cells had half the usual number of chromosomes.

The German biologist August Weismann suggested that the chromosomes were responsible for passing on the characteristics of the parents to the offspring. When a sperm and an egg joined together when fertilization took place, the offspring that resulted would have the full number of chromosomes, half from the mother and half from the father. Hugo de Vries, a Dutch botanist, worked out a theory that showed how different characteristics could vary independently of one another and could come together in many different combinations. In 1900, de Vries was ready to publish his work, but before he did so he checked carefully to see if anyone else had similar ideas. He was astonished to find that someone had. De Vries rediscovered the work of Gregor Mendel.

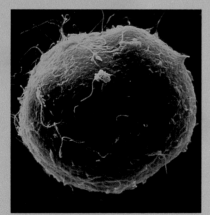

An egg cell surrounded by sperm. Egg and sperm cells have only half the usual number of chromosomes – an egg has to be fertilized by a sperm cell before it can grow.

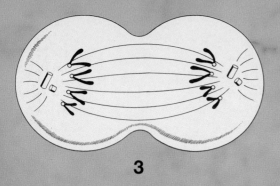

3

4

Gregor Mendel was a monk who lived in what is now the Czech Republic. He was fascinated by botany and for eight years, beginning in 1857, he grew peas in the monastery garden. He was particularly interested in discovering how characteristics such as flower color or height were passed on from one generation to the next. He discovered that each characteristic he investigated came in pairs – stems could be tall or short, seeds round or wrinkled, flowers purple or white, pods green or yellow, and so on. The pairs never mixed. A plant couldn't be medium-sized with green-and-yellow pods for example. On the other hand, a plant could have the different characteristics in any combination. The height of a plant didn't affect the color of its flowers. He also discovered that whatever gave the plant its particular characteristics came equally from the male parent and the female one. He called these factors of inheritance. In addition it seemed that, frequently, one of a pair of factors was dominant over the other. For example, if a plant got the factors for tallness from one parent and that for shortness from the other it would always be tall. A combination of tall and short characteristics never produced short plants. Shortness was said to be recessive.

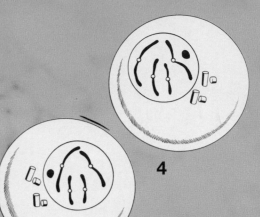

Gregor Mendel, the father of genetics. He was the first to show how characteristics could be passed on from one generation to another.

Mendel's peas

Mendel discovered that characteristics did not mix when different varieties were crossed. A pea with yellow seeds crossed with one with green seeds did not produce a plant with yellowy-green seeds. All of the offsprings' seeds were yellow. If the yellow-seeded offspring were crossed with one another their offspring had both yellow and green seeds. This showed that the green characteristic had not disappeared but had been hidden by the yellow characteristic. Yellow is said to be dominant over green for pea seed color.

Crossing yellow and green gives yellow seeds.

Crossing the yellow offspring gives yellow and green seeds.

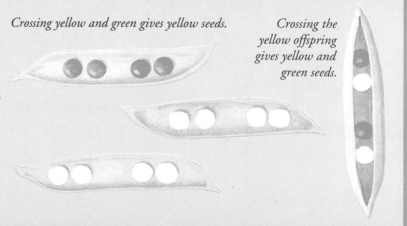

Humans come in a great variety of forms. The way we look comes from a combination of the characteristics we inherit from our parents and the environment we grow up in.

Mendel realized that most people would consider him to be just an amateur, so he tried to get the help of a well-known botanist in getting his work published. Unfortunately the man he sent it to, the Swiss botanist Karl von Nägeli, thought it worthless. Mendel's work was practically ignored, only being published in 1865 in an obscure journal where few people noticed it and none recognized its significance. So it remained until de Vries discovered Mendel's papers 35 years later. In fact, two other botanists, one in Germany and one in Austria, had also worked out the same ideas as de Vries, and they too had rediscovered Mendel's work. All three agreed that Mendel had got there first. They announced Mendel's work to the scientific world, saying only that their own research had confirmed it. Mendel got his credit at last, 16 years after his death.

If Mendel's work had been widely known in his lifetime Charles Darwin would have seen why the advantages different variations gave would be preserved and not lost as both animals and plants crossbred at random. Varying factors did not blend together but stayed separate. Natural selection could work on these variations and pick the ones that gave the best advantage.

This white bird is actually a blackbird! Its genes have given it white feathers rather than the more common black.

These are 23 human chromosomes taken from an egg cell. They have to combine with the 23 chromosomes in a sperm cell before a new human can grow.

Mendel's work was of great interest to biologists, who were particularly interested in discovering where the factors of inheritance were located in the cell. In 1909, the Danish botanist Wilhelm Johannsen suggested that they be called genes, from a Greek word that means "to give birth to." The idea was accepted. Later the English biologist William Bateson suggested the word genetics to describe the study of genes and inheritance. The father of genetics will always be Gregor Mendel, but Bateson was the first ever professor of genetics. He showed that Mendel wasn't entirely right and that some characteristics were inherited together, not independently. Some genes appeared to be linked.

The obvious place to look for the genes was in the chromosomes. After all, the way they divided and split up when sperm and eggs were being formed seemed to fit with Mendel's idea that each offspring got one of a pair of factors from the father and one from the mother. As there were only 23 pairs of chromosomes in a human cell, for example, and human beings had thousands of different characteristics, it must mean that each chromosome had thousands of genes. That would help to explain why some characteristics were linked. If the genes that caused them were on the same chromosome they would stay together.

Identical twins have exactly the same genetic information in their chromosomes. Slight differences in their appearance are caused by environmental factors.

Thomas Hunt Morgan's fruit fly experiments

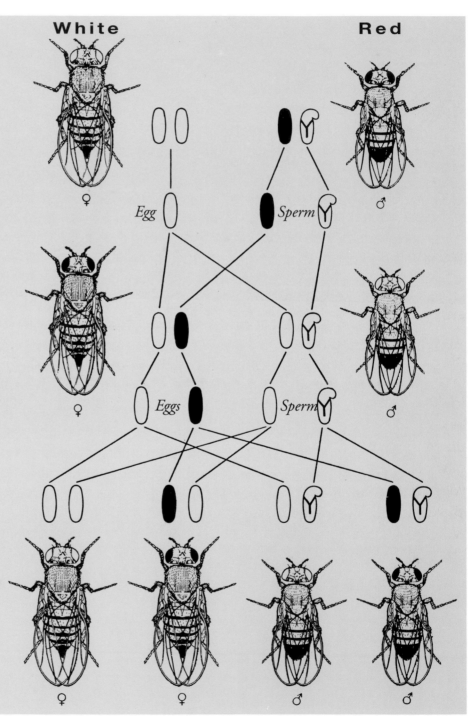

White **Red**

Egg *Sperm*

Eggs *Sperm*

M*any of the early breakthroughs in genetics were achieved through experiments carried out on the fruit fly (*Drosophila melanogaster*) by Thomas Hunt Morgan. The illustration here shows the results of crossing a white-eyed female with a red-eyed male. It is very similar to Mendel's pea crossing experiment. The female can only pass on genes for white eyes, but the male has genes for both white and red eyes. (The fact that the male actually has red eyes tells us that red is dominant over white.) If the offspring get white from the female and white from the male they will have white eyes. If they get white and red they will have red eyes.*

The white eye gene is also linked to the chromosome that decides whether or not the insect will be male or female (shown here as a Y). It was by studying linkages such as this that Morgan was able to determine where the fruit fly's genes were located.

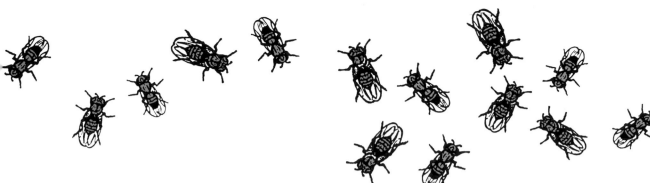

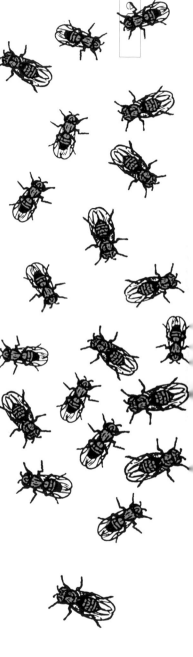

In 1907 Thomas Hunt Morgan, an American geneticist, started a series of experiments using the tiny fruit fly, *Drosophila melanogaster*. The advantages in using *Drosophila* were that it could be kept in large numbers very easily, it bred very quickly, and it only had four pairs of chromosomes. Morgan tried to establish the role of chromosomes by producing mutations in his fruit flies. De Vries had proposed that every so often a new variety of an organism might appear that was different in some respect from either of its parents. De Vries called these sudden changes mutations. Morgan failed to produce mutations artificially but he did find enough natural examples to be able to carry out his experiments.

Chromosome map

By following the mutations from generation to generation, Morgan showed that many characteristics were linked together, and therefore must be on the same chromosome. However, he observed that sometimes the linked characteristics could be inherited separately. It seemed that when the sex cells were being formed, pairs of chromosomes could exchange part of their length with each other so that linked pairs of genes might be split up. The greater the length of chromosome that separated the two genes, the greater was the chance that they would be separated when the chromosomes crossed over and exchanged material. By studying how often various linked pairs were split up, Morgan was able to begin drawing up the first chromosome map, showing roughly where the fruit fly's genes were.

So now it was known where the genes were, but how did they work?

CHAPTER SIX

In 1869 Johann Miescher, a Swiss biochemist, discovered nuclein. He gave it this name because it came from the cell nucleus.

The German chemist Albrecht Kossel set out to investigate nuclein more closely. He found that it was made of protein and nucleic acids, which were unlike any other substance that had been discovered in cells. Kossel discovered that the nucleic acids were made from five different nucleotides. These consisted of a chemical base attached to a sugar-phosphate group. The five chemical bases were called: adenine (A), cytosine (C), thymine (T), guanine (G) and uracil (U). In 1909, Phoebus Levene, a Russian-American chemist, showed that there were two types of nucleic acid. One was ribonucleic acid (RNA) and the other deoxyribonucleic acid (DNA). These were soon to be revealed as the most important components of life.

Genes and DNA

In 1944, O. T. Avery, a Canadian physician, demonstrated that physical characteristics could be passed from one type of bacteria to another. He was studying two of the bacteria that cause pneumonia. One had a smooth coat (S) and the other had a rough coat (R). He discovered that if he took an extract from dead S bacteria and mixed it with live R bacteria, he ended up with live S bacteria. The S extract obviously contained something that could convert R bacteria into S types. Avery determined that the extract contained DNA. This suggested that genes must be made of DNA. To discover how genes worked, and how exact copies of each gene were made every time a cell divided, it would be necessary to discover how DNA was structured.

Alexander Todd, a Scottish biochemist, carried on Levene's work and succeeded in making nucleotides in the laboratory.

Rosalind Franklin (1920–58) whose work on DNA was vital in determining its structure.

The structure of the nucleotides was now fairly well understood, but it was still not clear how they fitted together to form DNA and RNA molecules.

In 1944, the English biochemists Richard Synge and Archer Martin developed a method that made it possible to separate complex biological substances into simpler parts. Erwin Chargaff used their method to analyze DNA and discovered that DNA always contains the same number of adenine and thymine bases and cytosine and guanine bases.

By 1953, a way had been found using X-rays to distinguish the shape and structure of the DNA molecule. Extensive work was carried out by Maurice Wilkins, an English physicist, using this method. He showed that it had a regular shape. Rosalind Franklin, an English crystallographer, also carried out painstaking research on its structure.

James Watson (b.1928) and Francis Crick (b.1916) with their model of part of a DNA molecule in 1953. Watson is on the left.

The two people who made the breakthrough were the biochemists James D. Watson and Francis Crick. Crick and Watson started their work together on DNA in Cambridge in 1951. In autumn of that year, Watson attended a lecture given by Franklin. Along with Crick, he tried to use what he had learned to build a model of DNA. But the result was unsuccessful. There was more information needed before all the bits of the puzzle could be brought together.

In 1952, Watson and Crick met Chargaff when he visited Cambridge. He told them what he had discovered concerning the

The DNA molecule is remarkable in its ability to make exact copies of itself by unraveling and forming two daughter double helices. Each daughter helix has half of the original DNA's material; the rest is made up from material found in the cell.

DNA unravelling

paired numbers of bases in DNA. The full significance of this information wasn't understood at first. However, using the X-ray photographs of Franklin and Wilkins, it became clear that DNA was shaped like a helix or spiral. But the question remained as to how the nucleotides fitted together to give it this shape.

The answer came when Watson tried again to make a model of DNA. This time he used simple cardboard cutouts to represent the shapes of the bases. He discovered that an adenine-thymine pair was the same shape as the guanine-cytosine pair. Each pair of bases could be packed together regularly in the center of the helix. The regular pairing of the bases explained Chargaff's findings. Every cytosine had a guanine partner and every thymine was paired with an adenine.

In February 1953 Crick took over the model building. By the end of that month he had worked out how it all fitted together precisely. The DNA molecule was revealed as a double helix. The sugar-phosphate groups formed two spiraling backbones that twisted around the outside of the molecule and attached to the inside of these strands were the base pairs, like the steps of a spiral staircase.

The secret of DNA was revealed in the way the bases paired up. When Watson and Crick published their findings in the science journal *Nature*, they pointed out that the pairing of the bases could be the basis for making copies of the DNA. The first evidence for this came in 1958.

Two American scientists, Matthew Meselson and Franklin Stahl, were able to show that when a cell divides, half the original DNA ends up in one of the new cells and half in the other. Each new DNA helix has one old strand and one new one. The new ones are built up from the bases that exist freely in the cell. Because the bases have to pair up correctly, each new helix is exactly the same as the old

sugar phosphate

the bases paired up

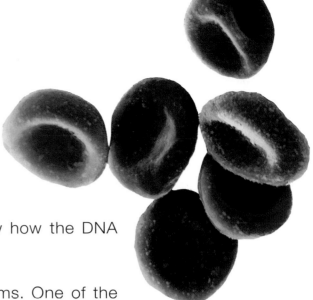

one. The next stage was for scientists to show how the DNA formed the genetic code.

RNA and proteins

Proteins perform various tasks in living organisms. One of the most important is controlling the many chemical reactions that go on in any living thing. Proteins that do this are called enzymes. Other proteins defend the organism against infection; transport substances around the body (such as the protein hemoglobin, that carries oxygen in the blood); allow muscles to move and nerves to send messages; and form the greater part of features such as hair, scales and feathers.

Each protein is made up of a long string of smaller units, called amino acids. There are 20 different kinds of amino acids and the order in which they appear in the protein determines what type of protein it will be. Each type of protein always has the amino acids in the same order.

The Central Dogma

Francis Crick continued to work on the way the genetic code might operate. He came up with something he called the Central Dogma. Put simply, this states that DNA makes RNA makes protein. This is how it works (see also the diagrams on page 42). A small section of the DNA molecule unravels into separate strands. Then nucleotides in the cell's nucleus align themselves against one of the strands, pairing up with the correct bases. Instead of a new DNA helix being formed, a single strand of special RNA (which is the other nucleic acid in the cell), called messenger RNA (or mRNA) is produced. In mRNA, the thymine base is replaced by the fifth nucleotide – uracil. After the mRNA has been formed, the helix joins up again.

The mRNA now leaves the nucleus and goes to the ribosomes. These are places inside a cell where proteins are made. Each group of three bases on the mRNA is called a codon and each codon is the code for a specific amino acid. The ribosome builds

Red blood cells transport oxygen from the lungs to the rest of the body. The oxygen is carried by binding it to the protein hemoglobin, which each red cell contains.

Making protein

1. *A section of the DNA molecule in the cell nucleus splits into separate strands. A molecule of messenger RNA (mRNA) is formed as nucleotides line up along one strand of the DNA.*

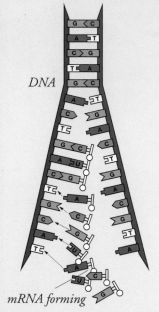

DNA

mRNA forming

2. *When the mRNA has been built up, the DNA reforms and the mRNA molecule leaves the cell's nucleus.*

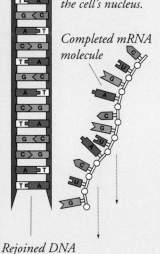

Completed mRNA molecule

Rejoined DNA

each protein step by step by reading the message on the mRNA that tells it which amino acids are needed. The ribosome moves along the mRNA so that each amino acid is matched against its codon and they join up in the correct order. It is possible for a number of different ribosomes to be moving along an mRNA chain at the same time, each building a protein as it goes. Here, at last, is the genetic code at work.

Amino acid molecules in the cell are brought to the ribosomes by another type of RNA, called transfer RNA (or tRNA), which is copied from the DNA. Every amino acid has its own specific tRNA. There is usually a supply of tRNA scattered throughout the cell.

Genes and mutations

The genetic code is common to practically all forms of life. A gene is a section of the DNA that carries the code to make a strand of RNA that will make a protein as described above. There are also control genes that control which sections of the DNA are copied by mRNA. So how does all this explain the different characteristics shown by a living organism? How does it all fit in with Mendel?

Take, for example, the pea with purple flowers. The color of the flower is determined by a pigment. The making of this pigment in the cells of the flower will have been controlled by an enzyme. An enzyme, you will recall, is a type of protein. The code for making a protein is found on part of the DNA – a gene!

3. *Molecules of transfer RNA (tRNA) bring amino acids to the mRNA to be assembled into proteins.*

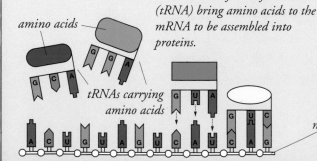

amino acids

tRNAs carrying amino acids

mRNA

4. *The tRNA molecules link up with the mRNA. Each amino acid has its own unique code that fits with part of the mRNA, so the protein is assembled in the right order. One by one, the amino acids are joined together and a protein is formed.*

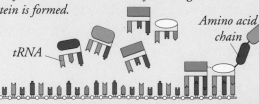

tRNA

Amino acid chain

The background on these pages shows a highly magnified photograph of ribosomes. These tiny structures are found in living cells and are the places where proteins are built up. This is done by using the information held on the DNA in the cell's nucleus.

DNA also provided an explanation for another very important characteristic of life on Earth, the fact that over time it changes, or evolves. Sometimes mistakes are made when the DNA is being copied (perhaps this might happen if the DNA is damaged in some way). If mistakes are made when the sex cells are being formed, the offspring will be different in some way from its parents. Most of the variations produced in this way by mutation will be harmful to the organism. Some, however, will be of benefit to it and give it an advantage over other members of its species. This might mean that it survives longer and has a better chance of reproducing and passing its advantage on to its offspring. This is the basis of evolution. Natural selection works on the random mutations that arise as DNA is copied, selecting those mutations that give an advantage. It is the final piece in Darwin's puzzle.

Glossary

Amino acid *Naturally occurring chemicals that are used by living organisms to build proteins. Plants and many microorganisms can make all the amino acids they need but animals must get them from food.*

Anatomy *The study of the structure of living organisms, especially the internal parts.*

Ancestor *An individual from whom others are descended and to whom a direct line can be traced through parents, grandparents, great-grandparents and so on.*

Bacteria *A group of single-celled microorganisms. Bacteria are found just about everywhere, both inside and outside other organisms. Bacteria play a major role in natural recycling processes. Diseases such as cholera, tetanus, tuberculosis and food poisoning are caused by bacteria.*

Biology *The study of living organisms, including their structure, their origins and evolution, where they live, and how they behave.*

Botanist *Someone involved in the scientific study of plants, which is called botany.*

Cell *The basic unit of living organisms. Cells can exist as independent life forms, such as bacteria, or may form tissues in more complicated organisms. Each cell has a central nucleus containing its DNA.*

Chromatin *A substance found in the nucleus of a cell, of which chromosomes are made. It contains proteins, DNA and RNA.*

Chromosome *Threadlike, coiled structures that become visible in the nucleus of cells when they divide. Chromosomes carry the genes that determine the characteristics of the organism. Each human cell has 46 chromosomes.*

Codon *A small part of DNA that determines which amino acid is needed when proteins are being made in a cell.*

Control gene *Parts of DNA that switch other genes on and off.*

DNA *Deoxyribonucleic acid, the genetic material of almost all living organisms. DNA consists of two long chains of nucleotides joined together and coiled into a shape something like a twisting ladder - the double helix.*

Descendant *An individual that has come from an earlier ancestor. For example, a child or grandchild.*

Dominant *The gene that controls a particular characteristic in an organism may have two forms.*

For example, the gene for height in a plant may be tall or short. The plant may have both forms, one from each parent. The form of the gene that actually decides the height is said to be dominant.

Element *A substance that cannot be broken down into a simpler substance by chemical means. There are 92 natural elements, including oxygen, hydrogen, nitrogen, carbon, iron and uranium.*

Environment *The biological, chemical and physical conditions in which an organism lives, its surroundings as a whole, including the influences of climate and other living organisms.*

Evolution *The gradual development of new plant and animal species from earlier forms of life over many millions of years. It is now widely believed that change comes about through natural selection, a view first put forward by Charles Darwin.*

Factors of inheritance *The name given by Gregor Mendel to the gene.*

Fossil *The remains or traces of an organism that existed in the past. Usually, only the hard parts, such as bones, shells and teeth, become fossils, though occasionally whole animals may be found. For example,*

the mammoths that have been uncovered frozen in the ice caps of Siberia and North America. Fossils generally occur where rocks have formed from the sediments of rivers, lakes or sea-beds.

Gene *The basic unit of inheritance, composed of DNA and forming part of a chromosome. Genes determine the particular characteristics of an organism that are inherited from its parents. They can have different forms (dominant and recessive) that determine how the characteristic is shown.*

Genetics *The study of the ways in which characteristics are passed from one generation to the next.*

Inheritance *That which is inherited, or passed on, from one generation to the next (height, eye color, skin color and so on).*

Microorganism *Any organism that can only be seen by using a microscope.*

Mitosis *A type of cell division in which two daughter cells are formed, each containing the same number and kind of chromosomes as the mother cell. This is the way in which body cells normally divide.*

Molecule *The smallest part of a chemical compound. Molecules consist of atoms of different elements.*

Mutation *A random change in part of the DNA of a cell that may cause it to look or behave differently from a normal cell. An organism affected by mutation is called a mutant. Most mutations are harmful, but any beneficial changes may be transmitted down the generations, ultimately leading to the evolution of a new species.*

Natural selection *According to Charles Darwin, this is the process by which new species appear. The offspring of a plant or animal that are best suited to their environment have the best chance of survival. The survivors pass on their advantages, which may come about through mutation, to their offspring. This results in a gradual change in the characteristics of the organism, eventually leading to the evolution of a new species.*

Nucleic acid *A complex chemical compound found in living cells. There are two types: DNA and RNA.*

Nucleus *A structure within a cell that contains its DNA.*

Organ *A part of an organism that performs a particular function. For example, an animal's organs include eyes (for seeing), lungs (for breathing), a heart (to move blood around the body), and so on. A plant's organs include its roots, leaves and flowers.*

Organism *An individual living thing.*

Ozone layer *Ozone is a form of oxygen that is created by the action of ultraviolet radiation. It is found in tiny quantities in the atmosphere, especially between 15 and 20 miles (20 and 25 km.) above the Earth's surface. This is the ozone layer. It absorbs most of the ultraviolet radiation from the sun, protecting living organisms on Earth from its harmful effects. This ozone shield is being damaged by air pollution.*

Photosynthesis *A process by which green plants and some types of bacteria convert simple molecules into complex compounds. It is the direct or indirect source of energy for nearly all forms of life. The energy of sunlight is used to drive a chemical reaction in which carbon dioxide gas from the atmosphere is combined with water to produce glucose, the simplest type of sugar, and oxygen. Almost all the oxygen in the atmosphere today has been produced by photosynthesis.*

Protein *One of a large group of compounds found in all living things. Proteins are made from long chains of amino acids, linked together in a specific order that is coded in DNA. One particularly important group of proteins, called enzymes, controls the rates at which activities take place in cells. The protein keratin gives strength and flexibility to hair, feathers and scales, and collagen does the same in skin and tendons. Proteins are an important part of muscles and are involved in the clotting of blood. A living organism may contain more than 10,000 different types of protein, all with a task to perform.*

Protista *Microorganisms that have a nucleus, as distinct from bacteria, which do not.*

RNA *Ribonucleic acid, a complex compound similar to DNA. RNA is formed in the cell nucleus by copying a section of DNA. There are three forms of RNA. Messenger RNA (mRNA) copies the part of the DNA that has the code for a protein. It takes this code to the ribosomes, where it is "read" by the ribosomal RNA. Molecules of transfer RNA (tRNA), each carrying a specific amino acid, are then brought into the correct positions along the messenger RNA to allow a protein to be made.*

Recessive *Opposite to dominant. Used in genetics to describe the form of a gene that does not have an effect when two different forms of the gene for a particular characteristic are present.*

Ribosome *A small spherical body, made of protein and a form of RNA, found within a living cell. This is where proteins are made by RNA.*

Species *A group of individual organisms, basically similar to one another, that are capable of breeding among themselves and producing fertile young. Polar bears, eagle owls and humans are all examples of species.*

Spontaneous generation *A now discredited belief that living things could arise naturally from nonliving materials.*

Stomata *Microscopic pores in the surface of leaves through which carbon dioxide enters to be used in photosynthesis and from which water vapor is lost. Individual stoma are opened and closed by guard cells on either side.*

Tissue *A group of similar cells organized together to perform a specific function for an organism, such as muscle tissue and nerve tissue.*

Virus *Simplest of all living things. A virus consists of a core nucleic acid, either DNA or RNA, surrounded by a protein coat. Viruses are totally dependent on living cells for their reproduction. The virus attaches itself to a cell and its nucleic acid enters the cell where it is replicated using material from the host cell. Protein coats are then assembled around the replicated nucleic acid and the cell is destroyed to release the new viruses. Some viruses can leave the host cell without destroying it. Viruses are frequently disease-causing agents, and are responsible for the common cold, influenza, herpes, polio, rabies and AIDS.*

Zoologist *Someone involved in the scientific study of animals, called zoology.*

Index

Numbers in bold indicate illustrations

Adenine bases 38, 39, 40, **42**

Amino acids 9, **9**, 41, 42, **42, 44**

Anatomy 24, 25-29, 44

Avery, O.T. 38

Bacteria 5-6, **5**, 10, 12, 26, 29, 38, 44

Bateson, William 35

Beagle, HMS 18-19, **19**

Beginning of life 8-15
  conditions for 8-10
  life on land 15
  ozone layer 12-15
  photosynthesis 10-12

Beneden, Edouard van 32

Bichat, Marie François 26-27

BIFs 11-12

Biology 4, 44

Blackbird **34**

Blood cells 41, **41**

Blood circulation 25

Brown, Robert 30, **30**

Buffon, Georges 16

Cells 5, 29, **31**, 41, 44
  blood 41, **41**
  discovering 26-27, **26**
  division 31-32, **32**
  (see also DNA; nuclei)

Central Dogma 41-42

Chargaff, Erwin 39, 40

Chromatin 30, 44

Chromosome maps 37

Chromosomes **30**, 30-33, **31, 32-3, 35**, 35-36, 44

Codons 41, 42, **42**, 44

Cohn, Ferdinand 29

Control genes 42, 44

Cork cells 26

Crick, Francis **39**, 39-41

Cyanobacteria 10

Cytologists 30

Cytosine bases 38, 39, 40, **42**

Darwin, Charles 18-23, **23**
  books 19-20
  natural selection 20-23

Darwin, Erasmus 16-17

De Vries, Hugo 32, 34

Deoxyribonucleic acid (see DNA)

Descent of Man, The 23

DNA (deoxyribonucleic acid) 7, 10, 38-43, **40**, **42**, 44

Dominant genes 33, **33**, 44

Double helix shape 40, **40**, 41

Drosophila melanogaster **36**, 37

Dyes (for studying cells) 30

Egg cells 32, **32**, **35**

Elements, basis of living things 9, 44

enzymes 41, 42

Essay on the Principle of Population, An 19-20

Evolution 16-23
  Charles Darwin 18-23

Factors of inheritance 33, 35, 44

Ferns **14**

Finches, Darwin's 18-19, **18**

Flemming, Walther 30-32

Forests, example of early **14**

Forms of life 4-7

Fossils **11**, **14**, **15**, 44

Franklin, Rosalind **39**, 39, 40

Fruit fly studies **30**, **36**, 37

Galápagos Islands 18, **18**

Galen 25, **25**

Genes 35, **36**, 37, 44
  and mutation 42-43

Genetics 35, 44

Germ theory of disease 29

Giraffes 17, **17**, 20-21

Glycine **9**

Guanine bases 38, 39, 40, **42**

Hemoglobin 41, **41**

Haldane, J.B.S. 9

Hooke, Robert 26, **26**

Hutton, James 16, **16**

Identical twins **35**

Inheritance factors 33, 35, 44

Insect breathing studies 25

Ironstone formations 11-12

Johanssen, Wilhelm 35

Kossel, Albrecht 38

Lamarck, Jean-Baptiste 17, **17**
Land, first life on 15
Leeuwenhoek, Antonie van 26, **26**
Levene, Phoebus 38

Maggots 28
Malpighi, Marcello 25-26
Malthus, Thomas 19-20, **20**
Martin, Archer 39
Mendel, Gregor 23, 32, 33-5, **33**, **35**
Messelson, Mathew 40
Messenger RNA (mRNA) 41-42, **42**
Microscopes 25, 26, **26**
Miescher, Johann 38
Miller, Stanley 9, **9**
Millipedes **15**
Mitosis 32, 44
Molecules 9-10, 13, 44
Morgan, Thomas Hunt **36**, 37
MRNA (messenger RNA) 41-42, **42**
Mutation 37, 42-43, 45

Nägeli, Karl von 34
Natural selection 10, 16, 20-23, 45
Naturalist's Voyage on the Beagle, A 19
Nuclei 30-37, **31**, 45 (see also DNA; RNA)
Nucleic acids 9, 38, **42**, 45 (see also DNA; RNA)
Nuclein 38
Nucleotides 38, 39, 40, 42,

On The Structure of the Human Body 25, **25**
Oparin, Aleksandr 9
Organs 24, 45
Origin of Species, The 22-23, **22**
Oxygen 11-12
Ozone layer 12-15, **13**, 45

Pasteur, Louis **28**, 29
Pea studies 33, **33**, 42,
Photosynthesis 10-12, 45
Proteins 41-42, **42**, 45
Protists 6, 45
Protozoa 26, 27

Radiation, ultraviolet (UV) 12-15, **12**, **13**

Recessive genes 33, **33**, 45
Redwood trees **4**
Ribonucleic acid (RNA) 38, 41-42, **42**, 43, 44
Ribosomes 42, **42-43**, 44
RNA (ribonucleic acid) 38, 41-42, 43, 45
Robots **7**
Rust 11

Schleiden, Matthias 27
Schwann, Theodor 27
Siebold, Karl 27
Single-celled organisms 27-28
Species 5, 45
Sperm cells 32, **32**, **35**
Spontaneous generation 27-28, 29, 45
Stahl, Franklin 40
Staining techniques 30
Stick insects 21, **21**
Stomata 26, 45
Structure of life 24-29
    discovering the cell 26-27
    germ theory 29
    single-celled organisms 27-28
Synge, Richard 39

Thymine bases 38, 39, 40, 42, **42**
Tissues 26-27, 45
Todd, Alexander 38-39
Transfer RNA (tRNA) 42, **42**, 43
Trilobites **15**
TRNA (transfer RNA) 42, **42**
Twins, identical **35**

Ultraviolet (UV) radiation 12-15, **12**, **13**
Uracil bases 38, 42, **42**

Vesalius, Andreas 25, **25**
Virchow, Rudolf 27-28,
Viruses 6-7, **7**, 42-43

Waldeyer, Heinrich 30
Wallace, Alfred Russel 22, **22**
Watson, James **39**, 30-40
Weismann, August 32
Whales **4-5**
Wilkins, Maurice 39, 40

X-ray diffraction 39

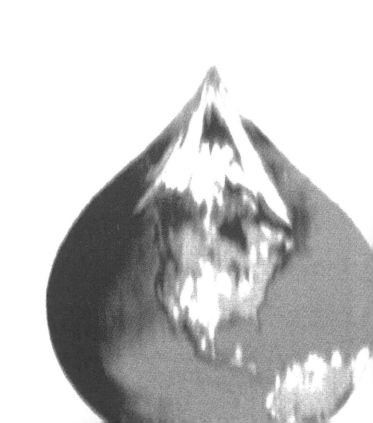